SEEING WITH OUR SOULS

SEEING WITH OUR SOULS

MONASTIC WISDOM
FOR EVERY DAY

JOAN CHITTISTER, O.S.B.

SHEED & WARD

Lanham, Chicago, New York, Toronto, and Oxford

Published by Sheed & Ward
An imprint of Rowman & Littlefield Publishers, Inc.
A wholly owned subsidary of The Rowman & Littlefield Publishing Group, Inc.
4501 Forbes Boulevard, Suite 200
Lanham, MD 20706

PO Box 317
Oxford
OX2 9RU, UK

Distributed by National Book Network

ISBN 1-58051-123-6

Cover and interior design: Madonna Gauding
Cover art used with permission from Super Stock

Printed in the United States of America.

*To Mary Miller, O.S.B., whose gift for seeing
has stretched my own soul*

Contents

INTRODUCTION

This time, like all times," Ralph Waldo Emerson wrote, "is a very good one, if we but know what to do with it." The answer to the tensions of humankind does not come from history. As the proverb teaches: time changes nothing; people do. The political, spiritual, economic, and cultural choices I myself make from day to day are the stuff of the next millennium. It is not the achievements of the past that a millennium appraises; it is the quality of our aspirations for the future that are in question now.

Seeing with our Souls will look at those qualities of the soul that must be cultivated by each of us if we are to become a different kind of people in this rapidly different kind of world. Cultures and countries and church communities are not made by institutional figures. They are made by us. The question is, What will we need to develop in ourselves if we ourselves are to be a positive presence in a changing world?

Vision

Proverbs 29:18

Where there is no vision the people perish.

I don't have a clue what led them to do it. The archives of women religious are, by and large, tombs of invisibility. Whatever few materials there are record decisions, not ideas, and definitely not the debates that led a group of women who had little or nothing to begin with to risk what little they did have for no advantage to themselves. Consequently, I can't explain why they did what they did. I only know that it may have been one of the six or so most determining acts of the community in our 144-year history.

In 1906 the small Benedictine community of women of which I am a part bought 140 acres of lakeside farmland for $10,000. It took the community years to pay it off. They never stepped foot on it, they never did a thing with it until, in 1930, they opened a children's camp on part of it as the community's response to the Great Depression. There were, of course, no utilities there. There were no main roads into it. They never farmed it or made any real profit out of it whatsoever. But they scrimped and saved to buy it anyway.

Today that property is the site of a Center that offers award-winning ecological programs, serves as a local conference center and gathering place, holds retreat programs year round, and, oh yes, that same children's camp has expanded now to include the poor, the handicapped, and the marginal, as well as children of families who can take this kind of thing for granted. That's vision.

Vision is not the ability to predict the future; it is a commitment to pursue possibility. Vision asks questions no one else even seems to know exist. Vision is the grace to evaluate the present and then to ask, Why not? of the future.

In a world where contaminated water is a child's worst enemy, where 44,000,000 people lack medical insurance in the richest nation of the world, where a government refuses to sign a nuclear nonproliferation treaty, where women everywhere are routinely denied the status of full human beings in both church and state, it is time to develop a new vision. It is time to ask, Why not? again. Not for our own sakes only, I learned from my foremothers, but for the sake of those who will come after us.

❧

The purpose of a millennium is not to measure the achievements of the past. It is to take the measure of our aspirations for the future. It isn't "progress," it's vision that counts.

❧

Vision depends on an ability to evaluate the present. It's one thing to want a better future—a lot of people do. It's another thing entirely to recognize what's lacking in the present so that we can, as a people, focus our energies on creating the kind of future that includes what we yet need but do not have.

❧

Never confuse desire with vision. Desire has to do with what we want. Vision has to do with what we need.

❧

Vision sees under the superficial to the central values of life. It is the compass point of the soul. It charts the way to the best in the human heart.

❧

"Without vision the people perish," Scripture says. When a people do not give serious thought to what they really need, they will get whatever anyone wants to sell them.

❧

The vision of a culture lies in what becomes its major institutions, in what it remembers as its most impacting events, in who it sees as its heroes.

❧

"I am in the world," Muriel Rukeyser says, "to change the world." Now that's vision. And who of us has the right to think otherwise?

❧

Vision is what I am willing to spend my life trying to make possible for others. To be devoted to nothing at all is to lack the vision it will take to make really living life for everyone.

❧

Vision is not the ability to predict the future. Vision is the foresight to create the future.

❧

Beware any vision of humanity that rests on the need to oppress any kind of it. After all, Hitler had a vision. Stalin had a vision. The cotton growers of the United States had a vision for their perfect world. The problem is that their vision for themselves left whole segments of the human community out of consideration.

❧

"The significance of human beings," Kahlil Gibran wrote, "does not lie in what we attain but rather in what we long to attain." It's what the heart desires, not what the hands grasp that determines a person's real value. That's why vision is a quality open to all: the rich as well as the poor, men as well as women.

❧

Vision is not the desire to do what we're already doing in bigger and better ways. We do economics well but the race for profit, without new vision, may well destroy us. We do freedom well but the lack of professional standards could certainly destroy us. We do personal development well but a lack of community consciousness could certainly degrade us as a people, as a nation. We need the kind of vision that tells us when to stop something as well as when to begin something.

❧

"Too low they build," Edward Young wrote, "who build beneath the stars." Setting our sights on what can be rather than learning to be satisfied with what is, is the seedbed of vision.

❧

Vision is the ability to take stock of where we're going by being brutally honest and relentlessly conscious of where we are. Vision isn't fortune-telling. It's the prophecy of possibility.

❧

"When we do not know what harbor we are making for," the Roman philosopher Seneca wrote, "no wind is the right wind." Persons have vision only when they have a dream that drives them on.

❧

To stumble from one thing to another in life, guided by nothing worth reaching for, going to nothing worth getting, is to waste the vision of the soul on the dying dreams of yesterday.

❧

Vision is what I have when I see a better way to do what has, for far too long, been done a lesser way. Vision is what makes life better for everyone.

❧

Someone with vision conceived of portable computers, food banks, democracy, and women's suffrage. And why did they work? Because so many others already shared the same vision. The question for this millennium is, What vision do we share now for the working poor, the elderly, the hungry of the world?

❧

Vision isn't the ability to create the impossible. "Vision," Jonathan Swift wrote, "is the art of seeing things invisible." Vision simply brings to consciousness what we all already know. That's why we recognize it once we hear it.

❧

It's knowing what questions to ask that constitutes vision.

❧

Susan Langer, the philosopher, wrote: "A philosophy is characterized more by the formulation of its problems than by its solution of them."

❧

Vision never takes the present for granted. Vision asks: Why are there homeless in the richest country in the world? Why are we putting money into nuclear weapons during peacetime when millions lack health care, children lack food, and our families lack child care? It's the questions we fail to ask that measure the paucity of our vision.

❧

Vision gives meaning to life. It propels us through difficulty when the goals we set are greater than the obstacles we must face in achieving them.

❧

Helen Keller wrote, "Many persons have a wrong idea of what constitutes true happiness. It is not attained through self-gratification but through fidelity to a worthy purpose." And Keller—the woman who could not see, could not hear, and could not speak, whose physical limitations changed the world for everyone—ought to know.

꙳

Doing more of the same isn't vision. It is simply the ability to tolerate the inadequacies of the present. It is at best a very mundane way to live.

꙳

People with vision are never satisfied with what is. They carry within themselves a holy agitation that leads them always to want more than being mediocre in anything can ever offer.

꙳

"Ideals are like stars," Carl Schurz wrote. "You will not succeed in touching them with your hands. But like seafarers on the desert of waters, you choose them as your guides, and following them you will reach your destiny." Ideals do not determine what we do to make a living in life; they govern what we become as we do it.

꙳

Ideals are formed in childhood. What are we encouraging our children to be, to do, to become in this society? Once we answer that question we will know clearly what the next century will be like.

꙳

A society without ideals is adrift: its leaders flounder; its children go soft; its people retire from the social fray or commit themselves to exploiting it. When military superiority and profit are the only ideals a country has left, don't you have to wonder what happened to that society's soul along the way?

꙳

Wayne Gretzky may know more about vision than he's likely to be given credit for. He said, "We miss 100 percent of the shots we never take."

A seeker searched for years to know the secret of achievement and success in human life. One night in a dream a sage appeared bearing the answer to the secret.

The sage said simply: "Stretch out your hand and reach what you can."

"No, it can't be that simple," the seeker said.

And the sage said softly, "You are right, it is something harder. It is this: Stretch out your hand and reach what you cannot."

Now that's vision.

An Understanding Heart

1 Kings 3:9

Give your servant, therefore,
an understanding heart.

I have lived in the inner city for a long time. It is not, by and large, a place of indiscriminate virtue. I have discovered that compassion comes no easier to the poor than it does to the rest of humankind. Compassion is clearly more a state of mind than a state of life. People are no more generous here, no more kind here, no more virtuous here than are people in the suburbs—despite the fact that they know suffering as few do. How can that be, I wondered? How is it that the poor do not commiserate with the poor? And then I understood: the poor know the burden of injustice, seldom the privilege of mercy. It is the advantaged who are called to compassion and mercy because it is the advantaged who have the luxury to give and the responsibility to understand.

I have known those things for a long time but yesterday I saw them alive and smiling. I met the young man in question in Cape Town, South Africa. He was from Chicago, heard the American accent, and took the trouble to tell me to "travel safely."

"I was beaten up on the street," he said, pointing to his half-healed right eye. "They stole the shoes right off my feet."

I winced a little.

"When I called to tell my mother," he said, "she was furious. But I said to her," he went on simply, "'Mom, you don't understand. Those shoes cost more than most of these people make in a year.'"

He smiled a little. "I just hope they fit him."

I realized that I had just seen real compassion in action. He understood the offense. He forgave the offender. He oozed no righteous fury. I learned a lot in that smile that I had known for years but, all of a sudden, knew differently.

❧

What we hold in our hearts for others is the way we'll act toward them. A hard heart makes for hard judgments; a compassionate heart understands the humanity of the one we presume to judge.

❧

Compassion for the other comes out of our ability to accept ourselves. Until we realize both our own weaknesses and our own privileges, we can never tolerate lack of status and depth of weakness in the other.

❧

The self-righteous hate themselves for their own weaknesses and so they despise them in others. That's why those who claim to be virtuous fall so much further, so much harder, than others when they fall. A touch of compassion for others along the way would surely soften the fall, as fall we shall—sooner or later.

❧

Compassion is the ability to understand how difficult it is for people to be the best of what they want to be at all times.

❧

Life buffets us at our best. That's why the hand of the one who understands our efforts, our errors, becomes the bridge that carries us over the failures of life.

❧

"What do you do in a monastery?" the seeker asked the monastic. "Oh, we fall and we get up; we fall and we get up; we fall and we get up." Perfection is not the absence of failure. It is the willingness to begin again and again.

❧

Compassion is the soft and bottomless well of the holy heart.

❧

To be like God is to open our arms wider and wider to those whose hearts are broken with the grief of their own inadequacies.

❧

"Judge not, lest you be judged," may not be the most ominous words in Scripture. It is the ability to accept the best in others as the best they have to give. After all, that's what gives us the right to fail ourselves.

❧

When we judge another, we ask God to hold us to the same unattainable standards that we have set for the rest of humankind.

❧

"Tsk, tsk" is a deadly habit. It closes the mind and sours the soul.

❧

"My feeling is that there is nothing in life but refraining from hurting others, and confronting those that are sad," Olive Schreiner wrote. The idea deserves thought. Imagine a world where "rugged individualism" and "natural corrections in the market place" gave way to "refraining from hurting the others and comforting those who are sad." National compassion would surely mean no more street people. No more children with nowhere to go. No more hungry people in the richest country in the world. More welfare for the poor as well as for the rich.

❧

Compassion is the virtue that opens heaven to us. It is what makes us most like God.

❧

Everyone suffers in life. Compassion is that quality in another that makes it possible for us to survive it.

❧

Compassion makes no distinction between friends and enemies, neighbors and outsiders, compatriots and foreigners. Compassion is the gate to human community.

❧

Compassion is not sympathy. Compassion is mercy. It is a commitment to take responsibility for the suffering of others.

❧

"Even the little pigs grunt," Selma Lagerlof wrote, "when the old boar suffers." To empathize with the suffering of another is the sign of the person who is capable of caring for something besides the self. Narcissism is an affliction of the small-minded; compassion is the hallmark of the great of soul.

❧

Compassion is not the natural order of things. The natural order of things starts with me. The supernatural order of things starts with those for whom the natural order of things is not enough. "When a person has pity on all living creatures then only are they noble," the Buddha said. That's why compassion has so long been the real mark of sanctity.

❧

"We hand folks over to God's mercy," George Eliot wrote, "and show none ourselves." But God who lives in us, waiting to be released into the world, expects us to do more than that.

❧

Compassion is the only thing we have that merits us mercy. Otherwise, on what grounds do we expect what we do not give?

❧

"Compassion is the antitoxin of the soul," Eric Hoffer wrote. "Where there is compassion even the most poisonous impulses remain relatively harmless." To care for the other is not only to do them no harm; it is the unrelenting intention to do them nothing but good. And once that starts, how can any other evil enter the heart?

❧

It's one thing to do good; it's another thing to be good. It's possible, perhaps, to do good simply out of principle, but it's impossible to really be good that way—not if goodness is a quality of the heart and not simply an exercise of the will.

❧

God is compassion. "I have heard the cry of my people," Yahweh says in Exodus, "and I mean to deliver them." The basic spiritual question of life may be "Whose cries do we hear and what have we done to deliver them?"

❧

To be without compassion is to fail to know the self. When we recognize and accept our own frailties, we have no trouble dealing tenderly with the needs and the lapses of others.

❧

Compassion is the sacrament of concern. To the person who is compassionate, tragedy is not a news report. It is a call to respond.

❧

I always wonder why it is that we ask whether a candidate for the presidency is tough enough to push the nuclear button but we never ask if they are strong enough not to. I can't help but wonder if that might not have something to do with the Compassion Quotient of contemporary culture.

❧

A woman invited some people to dinner. At the table, she turned to her six-year-old daughter and said, "Would you like to say the blessing for us, dear?" But the little girl said, "I wouldn't know what to say." "Well, just say what you hear Mommy saying, darling," the woman prodded her. So the little daughter shrugged her shoulders, bowed her head, and said: "Dear God, why on earth did I invite all these people to dinner?" Point: Compassion may not be the easiest thing in the world to explain to someone but it always has more effect than protocol ever will.

❧

Compassion is not indifference to sin; it is the understanding of how sin happens to the best of us, including you and me.

❧

When another person is suffering and I do not suffer as well, I pretend that I am God. When another person is suffering and I suffer with that person, I admit that I, too, am only human.

Humility

1 Peter 5:5

All of you should wrap yourselves
in the garment of humility.

I travel enough to know that to be an American outside of America is to carry a very heavy social burden. Stereotypes plague us every step of the way: Americans, the conventional wisdom implies, are rich, aggressive, loud, uncouth, and unlettered but they are, at the same time, these international pundits maintain, powerful, generous, and—in contradistinction to their European or Eastern counterparts—pragmatic rather than philosophical. We're effective, in other words, but arrogant. Upstarts with a lot to learn. Crude in our social graces, boorish in our politics, self-centered and self-satisfying. Whew.

The truth is that the assessments aren't all wrong. We have, after all, invented the end of the world and we say we're willing to use it. That's at least uncouth. We have developed a very high standard of living but a great deal of it has been at the expense of those who do our dirty work for slave wages. That's certainly arrogant. We have bartered a tradition of liberal arts education for the sake of the technical. That's pragmatism to the ultimate.

And yet, on the other hand, we give more per capita to charity than any other people on earth. We have made science, medicine, and interplanetary exploration high art. We have managed to recognize the civil rights and personal freedoms of every person in the country, regardless of race or religion.

And, oh yes, one more thing. We may have a bit of humility, too, that isn't apparent, unless, of course, you know what humility really is. About six years ago, I stepped into a waiting cab in another country a few minutes later than the time I'd ordered it. "I'm so sorry, sir," I said to the driver. "I was on the phone when you drove up."

I became aware as we crossed the city that the driver was watching me closely through the rearview mirror. Finally, he said to me, "You're an American, aren't you?"

"I am," I said. "How did you know?"

"Well, ma'am," the man said, "I've been driving this cab for thirty-two years and no one has ever called me 'sir' before. But you Americans are like that. You support one another in everything. We don't do that here. Here we get ahead by making sure that everyone else knows they're lower than we are."

I smiled. Here was a holy man who knew down deep that humility had nothing to do with personal diminishment. Real humility, this wise man knew, was the process of being everything you could possibly be—and helping everybody else be their best, too.

The word *humility* comes from *humus*, the Latin word for "earth." A person who is humble, in other words, knows the stuff—earth—of which they're made: a talent here, a weakness there, a degree of competency here, a blunder there. Humble persons know what they are and what they aren't, what they have and what they don't have, and they never confuse the two.

There is no soil that grows everything. The earth that is fit to cultivate roses is not fit to grow vineyards. But that doesn't mean that it's not good earth. Humility requires that I develop what I am rather than pretend to be what I am not.

Humility is the ability to recognize the glory in the clay of me.

"Without humility there can be no humanity," John Buchan wrote. When I know and accept myself—all my strengths and all my limitations—I am immediately respectful of everyone else because, I know, they have something beautiful within them that I do not have.

Only those are unhappy who are trying to be what they are not.

Humble persons are seldom frustrated and never in despair. They never for a minute think that the world was made to revolve around them or that they have the power to make it do otherwise. So when things to not go according to their tiny little plans, it never surprises them.

❧

Humble persons give all their special gifts away—their ideas, their time, their presence—and are genuinely surprised to discover that other people really want them.

❧

It's Ash Wednesday in the Christian world. It is the feast day of humility. "Remember that you are dust," the minister says while putting ashes on the forehead of each, "and unto dust you shall return." Remember, in other words, of what you are made and then, without doubt, having come to accept yourself, you will open your arms to the rest of the world.

❧

Humility is the world's antidote to self-righteousness. Self-righteousness is the disease that assumes that if I say so, it must be so and if I want it, I ought to have it. A lot of wars, domestic and otherwise, could be prevented with the slightest touch of humility.

❧

Humility and humiliation are not the same. Humiliation diminishes a person, leaves the person ashamed and hurt and angry. Humiliation is a negative thing that always comes back in negative ways. Humility gives a person the insight it takes to value others and develop the self.

❧

Humility brings persons to a realistic assessment of their abilities and in that way frees them to do with them what is doable, not what is not.

❧

The person who is humble is the person who is secure. When I know of what I'm capable, I never have to compete with anyone to be anything else. Horace Mann wrote, "To know all things is not permitted." Think of it: My inadequacy is what makes for human community.

❧

"To make your children capable of honesty," John Ruskin wrote, "is the beginning of education." It's not learning to deny our talents that is the essence of humility. It's learning that we don't have them all that is the real gift of humility to the world.

❧

"If you wish your merit to be known," an Oriental proverb teaches, "acknowledge that of other people." Humility is the ability to recognize the gifts of others in such a way that they are free to recognize our own without fear of being swallowed up in the clamor of our wake.

❧

We're not here to suppress the gifts of others in order to make room for our own. We're here to put all the gifts of humankind into the great pool of humanity so that, because of the gifts of each of us, we can all live better in the end.

❧

Walter Lippman calls humility "the saving doubt of our own certainty." In fact, are we ever more wrong than when we are certain we are right? Humility allows us the sliver of possibility that we may still learn something.

❧

Humility saves us from the terminal disease of self-centeredness. It enables us to be comfortable with who we are so that we can be comfortable with whom everyone else is, too.

❧

"Nothing is more deceitful," Jane Austen wrote, "than the appearance of humility. It is often only carelessness of opinion, and sometimes an indirect boast." Or to put it another way: "See how humble I am" is, in other words, a square circle. Real humility is not an "appearance." It is a state of mind that says I am only what I am. Nothing more. Nothing less. And you are the rest of what is good in life.

❧

"If you bow at all, bow low," the Chinese proverb reads. It's an important insight. Deference—bowing to the will of another—and humility—bowing to the God within them—are not the same thing. Deference is the mark of those who exalt another; humility is the mark of those who revere another.

❧

Humility leads me to do anything I can do in any situation without having to do everything in every situation.

❧

The Rule of Benedict, a spiritual document that is now fourteen centuries old, says that there are twelve characteristics of humility. The first characteristic is the awareness that I am not my own god, that there is a power above and beyond me by whose power I live. In a scientific age, when the old myths about a God who sits on clouds watching people are falling away, the idea of the God of Life is even more powerful, more humbling.

❧

The second element of humility, according to the Rule of Benedict, is the awareness that God's will for me—those circumstances over which I have no control—may at first seem bad for me but will, in the end, be for my good. Humility gives me spiritual insight into what, at first, is not seeable.

꙳

The third element of humility is the ability to recognize that others may know just as well, and even better sometimes, what ought to be done in any given situation and to accept their direction. It brings us to reverence the insights of others. It frees us from the need to hoard power.

꙳

The fourth element of humility, Benedict says, is to realize that when we find ourselves under the power of others, everything in life will not be easy, that others will do things differently, and that it may not be to our liking. But that doesn't make it wrong. It simply makes it one more lesson in life that we clearly need to learn.

꙳

The fifth element of humility is to seek the counsel of others and to reveal oneself honestly to those persons who can help us become our best selves. Humility is the ability to take off the masks we wear in public so that we can put down the heavy burdens of having to pretend to be smarter, richer, holier, or stronger than other people. "You never find yourself," Pearl Bailey said, "until you face the truth."

꙳

The sixth element of humility, Benedict says, is to be content with less than the best. Humility is what enables us to accept natural circumstances—the fact that we are not as rich as the neighbors, that our siblings are better placed than we are, that we don't have the newest car on the block. Humble people do not have nervous breakdowns when it rains on picnic day.

꙳

The seventh characteristic of the truly humble person is the ability to accept criticism, to go through life prepared to change and change again, to know that we have not yet arrived. "Let us accept truth," George Sand wrote, "even when it surprises us and alters our views." There is always more and more and more to learn from others.

⁂

The eighth characteristic of humility is that humble people have the ability to learn from those who have gone before them. They have a genuine reverence for the elderly, a great love of the young. They "learn from the community," as Benedict says. They are not oracles unto themselves. Humility is acceptance of the self and openness to others. It is a very freeing thing.

⁂

The ninth, tenth, and eleventh characteristics of humility are the ability to keep silence, to speak gently, and to avoid the ridicule of others. The person who has every answer, who consumes all the air in a conversation, and who disparages his or her fellow human beings uses speech to batter others into submission. Soft speech is the mark of the person who reveres the other. It turns cab drivers into "sir."

⁂

The twelfth characteristic of the humble person is serenity. When we accept the self, reverence the other, and learn that what cannot be changed must be accepted for what it is, we have learned the secret of living with ease, with hope, and with joy. Humility is the virtue of the daily.

⁂

"I'm not offended by all the dumb blonde jokes," Dolly Parton said. "In the first place, I know I'm not dumb . . . and in the second place, I also know that I'm not blonde." Now that's humility.

Soul

Matthew 10:28

Do not fear those who deprive the body of life
but cannot destroy the soul.

S oul is hard to find. We talk about it a lot but we don't really know what it is. Personality we describe with a certain amount of confidence. Intelligence we measure regularly. Feelings we understand and explore with ease. But "soul"? Soul seems to escape us entirely. Soul is one of the intangibles of life. It's one of those things that we only recognize when we see it. But it's possible that we see it a great deal more than we realize. At least we get glimpses of it everywhere. I know for sure I saw it once, and just where I would never have expected.

Every year our community holds a public "giveaway." It's held in the parking lot of the community soup kitchen that is located in the heart of the inner city. The items available "for sale" come from the sisters themselves. As part of the community Lenten preparation, each of us gives up something we have and like for someone who would need it or like it more. The things that appear in the Lenten box are good things— new, barely used, or completely refurbished—but whatever their condition, they are all basically practical articles: a new sweater, an old pen set, a jacket outgrown, a scarf that's still in its gift box. And a few isolated things on the side that defy categorization, of course: a harmonica, maybe, or a teddy bear or a pair of dumbbells or a cut glass vase.

On the appointed day, every guest at the soup kitchen gets a "coupon book" of six tickets to spend at the tables in the parking lot outside. The tables that year were heaped: two tables full of women's blouses, of course, one table full of shoes, one table full of coats, a small table full of knickknacks, and, over against the fence at the far end of the parking lot, stack after stack of pictures. Pictures of everything: the Grand Canyon, Niagara Falls, tulips, sunsets, country scenes, the lake, whatever. Pictures. Hundreds of pictures taken right off bedroom walls. "Good heavens," I thought a little testily. "Who donated those? Nobody is going to want that kind of stuff. How are we ever going to get rid of those things when this is over?"

But when I looked up from the coat table twenty minutes later, most of the coats were still there but all the pictures were gone. Not one was left. Up and down the street as far as the eye could see there were old women in sneakers, young women with children, and men in jeans carrying away pictures the size of a fireplace lintel.

Why? I wondered, with no small amount of chagrin. Why would they want pictures? And then I knew: it's called "soul" and you often miss it in sneakers and jeans, and you can't satisfy it on food stamps.

❧

Soul is that extra something we bring to life that gives us the capacity to appreciate it.

❧

"Live all you can," Henry James said. "It's a mistake not to. It doesn't so much matter what you do in particular, so long as you have your life. If you haven't had that, what have you had?" It's not a question of having a job or having a nice house. The question is, Have you had a life? Are you full of soul or do you just have a body?

❧

Soul is music and art and fun and love and new ideas and pause. It doesn't come prepackaged. You have to cultivate it. But once you do, no amount of death can take it away from you.

❧

When you see something in a situation that no one else has seen, when you hear a chord in the music that you have never heard before, when you read a line and think about it all day long—that's soul. It's the way we know we're still alive. Not "living." Alive.

❧

Life is a recipe made up of multiple ingredients and various seasonings that are meant to simmer. It can't be rushed; it can't be ignored. It must be tasted regularly. That's soul.

❧

It's so easy to confuse desire with soul. Desire is to want what we don't have. Soul is what enables us to draw the best out of what we do have.

❧

"For the benefit of the flowers," the Jewish saying teaches, "we water the thorns, too." Nothing comes to us without cost. Nothing comes to us wholly good or wholly bad. Soul is what enables us to bear one and celebrate the other.

❧

Soul is the ability to stretch ourselves—our language, our thoughts, our responses, our reactions—one notch higher than our present circumstances seem to require.

❧

How do we know whether or not we have soul? Easy. All we have to do is ask ourselves what it is that makes our juices flow. You do still have juice, don't you? Just listen to yourself and you'll know. "Some people's hearts are shrunk in them, like dried nuts," Douglas Jerrold said. "You can hear 'em rattle as they walk."

❧

It's not stress and involvement, it's not being busy, that destroys us. It's when life ceases to engage us, when getting up in the morning is more burden—more boring—than it is a challenge, that the sign is clear: something is draining the soul out of us.

❧

Soul is what gives us the life energy that carries us through the mundane of the daily to the most meaningful dimensions of life. The problem is not that we didn't get enough soul to make life meaningful; the problem is that soul is what we are required to nurture in ourselves. All we get is the raw material to make one.

❧

Soul is what enables us to respond, to give to every moment what it deserves. Or as Golda Meir said: "Those who don't know how to weep with their whole heart don't know how to laugh either."

❧

Being "cool" is the opposite of having soul. When we fail to enter into every moment to the ultimate, we withhold ourselves from the experience. And the experience withholds itself from us, too.

❧

Showing some soul in life is not weakness. It is truth. The Yiddish saying teaches: "People do not fall because they are weak, but because they think themselves strong."

❧

Soul seeks the intangibles of life: fun at a party, beauty in the home, courage in the face of disapproval. It lives life to the hilt. "We have had too much talk of sheep," Teilhard de Chardin wrote. "I want to see the lions come out."

❧

How do you get soul? Just do it. Whatever you're doing, do it with everything you have. Sarah Bernhardt said, "Life engenders life. Energy creates energy. It is by spending oneself that one becomes rich."

❧

If you're depressed because you see everyone around you living more fully than you are, it may be because you are waiting for life to come to you rather than your going to it. Take life on. That's soul.

❧

The interesting thing about soul is that in order to get it, you have to have it. Or, as the ancients said, "If you bring forth what is within you, what you bring forth will save you."

❧

It's so seductive to live life passively. All you have to do is sit back and see what happens. You don't engage. You don't participate. You don't get involved. You sit back and yawn. Or you sit back and criticize everybody who is engaged, who is participating, who is involved.

❧

I saw a card a few days ago. The cover read, "You and I have a unique and beautiful relationship." Inside it said, "You are unique and I'm beautiful." Now that kind of *chutzpah,* I thought, is the raw material of soul.

❧

The Spanish say, "Those that lose wealth, lose much; those that lose friends, lose more; but those that lose spirit, lose all." Funny how many people lose money and think that life itself is lost; lose their friends and never get over it; lose their spirit and call it either growing up or old age. Sad.

❧

Today a woman told me that she doesn't hang her diploma in her office. She hangs her library card instead. "That's the most important membership I ever got," she says. "That's what really changed my life." That's soul, too.

❧

Life is only as wide and as deep as our souls are. If we've been weaned on littleness, life will be little for us. But if we have been nursed on great ideas, great experiences, great beauty, and great awareness, life will have no limits.

❧

The amount of spirit we bring to life is the amount of spirit we will get out of it.

❧

Soul is what's left over after everything else in life seems to be lost. George Orwell put it this way:

The thing that I saw in your face
no power can disinherit;
No bomb that ever burst
Shatters the crystal spirit.

❧

One of the things that dampens soul is pseudo-sophistication, the need to look like something we're not so people will think we're more detached, more disinterested, more superior to the situation than we really are—or would like to be. So, let go for a change, why don't you. After all, you've got nothing to lose but your soul.

❧

"The great," Ralph Waldo Emerson said, "are they who see that the spiritual is stronger than any material force." That assumes, of course, that the spiritual has been developed in the first place.

❧

"There's plenty of fire in the coldest flint," Rachel Field said. Soul is in all of us. It's just a matter of letting it bubble to the top. The real question is not, Why don't I have soul? The real question is, Why don't I trust it more?

❧

The joy of life doesn't come "whole." It comes in diamond chips. The trouble is that it takes soul to find diamond chips in the dark.

❧

There are too many people trying to get into heaven who have yet to muster the amount of soul it takes to appreciate all the life there is on earth.

HOLY INDIFFERENCE

Matthew 6:26

*Look at the birds in the sky. They do not sow or
reap, they gather nothing into barns;
yet our God in heaven feeds them.*

If there is anything that strikes terror into the soul of the sincere it is fear of failure. To be a success in something marks the measure of our worth. It gives us honor on the street corners of our worlds. It gives us stature among our peers. It gives us a sense of invincibility. But one of the central questions of life may well be how to tell success from failure. It's not so simple a task as we are inclined to think, perhaps, at the first toss of the question. Failure, we know, is unacceptable. We do a great deal to avoid it. We do even more to hide it. But the real truth is that there is a great deal of failure in all success: Winning pitchers lose a good many baseball games. Wealthy people risk a great deal of money to make money. Scientists can spend their entire lives mixing the wrong compounds, writing the wrong formulas, testing the wrong hypotheses.

The problem is that there are two faces of failure, one of them life-giving, the other one deadly. I have seen them both.

The first face of failure I saw in the life of an internationally recognized writer who, first intent on being an English professor, studied at Oxford but failed. I gasped at the very thought of it. But she spoke about the loss of those years and that degree with a laugh and a toss of her head: "Luckiest thing that ever happened to me," she said. "Otherwise I'd be in a small college someplace teaching writing. As it is, I'm doing just what I'm supposed to be doing." I thought about the remark for days. Here was a woman who knew the place of failure in our eternal quest to be ourselves.

The second face of failure I saw in a woman with great musical talent who, discouraged by the difficulty of her early studies, dropped out of music school and never studied another thing in her life. She died disgruntled, underdeveloped, and trapped within the boundaries of the self.

Clearly, failure may, in the long run, be the only real key to success. The first step to becoming what we most seek may well be indifference to dashed hope and perpetual disappointment and the depression that comes with reaching for guinea gold and grasping only dust.

But if that is the case, then we must develop the capacity for failure in a society that glorifies success but gives short shrift to the forging of it. We must learn to recognize, to value, to prize all the endless attempts it takes to do what we want to do but which for us is still undoable.

We need to cultivate a sense of holy indifference.

❧

Failure is simply the opportunity to begin again.

❧

Those who know how to fail and survive it are those who know how to succeed.

❧

There is no such thing as failure for those who see the seeking as important a part of the process as the chance to become what they seek.

❧

Holy indifference to failure is the capacity to bleed every moment for what it is in itself rather than to stake our entire lives simply on the applause of the system that generated it. Otherwise we will do nothing in our lives just for the joy of doing it but only for the approval of those in whose presence we do it. That's called "playing to the audience."

❧

Those only succeed who have been willing to fail often enough to deserve it.

❧

Don't be ashamed of failing. Only be ashamed of what you have refused to try for fear of failing. If a thing is worth succeeding at, it is worth failing in the process.

❧

There's no such thing as instant success. The Spanish proverb teaches: "However early you get up, you cannot hasten the dawn."

❧

To be destroyed by failure is to give in to the part of the self that wants glory without having to climb all the way to the summit to earn the view.

❧

To have the character to fail is to have the character to succeed at something else.

❧

We have so confused the norms of success in this society that we no longer know failure when we see it. People who could have earned more money had they chosen to spend more time at the office and less time with the family; people who could have been more socially prominent had they just been willing to forego old friends from old neighborhoods; people who could have lived in more sophisticated cities had they been willing to give up fishing and walking in the woods: these people we consider some kind of social failures. But maybe what they really succeeded at becoming was real people instead of hollow copies of advertising models for *Lifestyles of the Rich and Famous*.

❧

Becoming what we really are instead of what someone else says we should be is life's final success story.

❧

Life is too short to squander on any success that is not bought at the price of regular failure. In any other case, what we gain may not be worth the gaining.

❧

"One life," Carlyle wrote, "a little gleam of Time between two Eternities." When it's over, it's over. Then, all anybody will wonder is whether or not we succeeded in being the most fully and lovingly human model of whatever we finally are.

❧

Failure is not a condition. It is a state of mind. Thaddeus Golas says it well: "Inside yourself or outside, you never have to change what you see, only the way you see it."

❧

When we poison ourselves with the need to surpass others rather than to surpass ourselves, we lose the very essence of success.

❧

Failure is the lodestar that guides us beyond the commonplace of ourselves. Hermann Hesse reminds us: "We have to stumble through so much dirt and humbug before we reach home. And we have no one to guide us. Our only guide is our homesickness." To be told that we have failed is to be told what we are capable of being when we finally find the thing that makes all our stumbling attempts at it worthwhile.

❧

To become paralyzed by failure is to give in to death before we have even begun to live.

❧

When what we thought we wanted is impossible to attain, it is time to change our idea of what we want.

❧

The end of life is crowned by the amount of effort we put into it. "We are all failures," J. M. Barrie wrote. "At least, all the best of us are."

❧

Success has a great deal more to do with being than gaining. Whatever we gain can be taken away from us by those who give it to us or those who take it away. But real success rests on what we become that is not given to us by anyone but ourselves.

❧

Samuel Beckett said it best in *Worstward Ho*: "Ever tried. Ever failed. No matter. Try again. Fail again. Fail better." Without failure what we want most to be in life can never succeed.

❧

If we have never stretched ourselves to the level of failure, we have certainly never really done anything that we can call a success.

❧

The ability to fail is what gives us the right, as Robert Frost says, "to look backward with pride . . . and forward with hope." But fail we must. Without holy indifference to failure, we can never really experience success.

❧

When we can take failure without emotional collapse or public shame—when we can learn to laugh at the level to which we've come and the distance that we've yet to go—life has become one long exercise in the joy of living.

❧

"The world," Francis Picabia wrote, "is divided into two categories: failures and unknowns." Any success that comes without failure is not success at all. It is simply doing what comes naturally. It's doing more than what we can do without effort that, in the end, really measures our mark.

❧

In everybody's life there is something that we want to do more than we want to do anything else. The only question is whether what we want to do is what we can do and whether what we can do we are giving enough effort to doing.

Anything else is either tragic misunderstanding of the self or a comedic misuse of a natural gift.

❧

Dilettantes are people who succeed superficially at a lot of things by refusing to fail at any of them.

❧

Real failure comes when we consider ourselves good enough at something to be able to repeat it rather than to develop it. "Success is dangerous," the painter Pablo Picasso said. "One begins to copy oneself, and to copy oneself is more dangerous than to copy others. It leads to sterility."

❧

Beware of your definition of success: If it has more to do with what other people think of you than it does with what you know of your own abilities, you may be confusing applause with achievement.

❧

Failure is simply another turn in the road. There are many ways to the top of the mountain. The important thing is simply to keep trying until you get there—by one path or another.

❧

"Failure after long perseverance," George Eliot wrote, "is much grander than never to have a striving good enough to be called a failure." Pity those who have never failed. You have to wonder if they ever tried anything hard enough to find out what they could really have done in life if they had been brave enough to fail at it.

Gentleness of Spirit

Philippians 4:11

For I have learned, in whatsoever state I am,
therewith to be content.

For months, the papers had been full of stories about road rage and football brawls and children who have been beaten because they "wouldn't stop crying." I was exhausted by the weight of such perpetual violence but the feel of it had become so much a part of the urban landscape that I myself was feeling pretty dulled to the whole situation. Or at least I thought I was until I took a foreign visitor on a trip through downtown U.S.A.

The woman was an Australian—one of those friendly, very laid-back types of Aussies who amble down the beaches of life smiling. We were on our way to return the most recent home movie rentals. It was a bitterly cold and snowy day in the Midwest. Ice was forming under us as we drove. As the traffic neared the Video Barn I said the American thing: "I'll slow down at the corner, you jump out with the video, and I'll keep going around the block till you come back out." Simple. Routine. We do it all the time.

Not this time.

The light turned red. She got out of the car, stood at the curbside, looked for money in her wallet, closed up the wallet again, stacked it carefully against the back of the seat, pulled her collar up, her jacket down, her sleeves into place, closed the door—twice—and started toward the back of the car. The light turned green. I looked up at the long line of traffic forming behind us. "Oh, no," I thought. "The video is on the back seat." She opened the back door of the car and rustled carefully through a stack or two of books. The cars behind me inched up to the bumper.

"Gail," I said. "Hurry. There's a line of traffic behind us." She looked around slowly, frowned at me a little, and said, "Well, that's all right. They'll wait." The light turned red again. I took in a deep breath and realized that my hands were tight on the wheel.

When she got back into the car after returning the video, I paused a minute and said, "Gail, listen to me. The next time

I let you out in traffic, just jump and run. This is a very fast-paced country. Therefore, it is often a very short-tempered country. Sometimes people even get violent about having to miss green lights." I could see the look on her face: very thoughtful, very disturbed. "What do they gain by that?" she said. Pause action.

The short answer is, "Nothing." The long answer is a study in the psychology of false stress. More than that, it may be a study in a very superficial spirituality. Or as Harriet Beecher Ward said once, "Americans go very deeply into the surface of things." When we are embedded in life at its depths, we develop gentleness of spirit. No amount of trivia can unsettle equanimity of soul.

❧

Real spirituality has something to do with not getting disturbed about anything that is not worth getting disturbed about. It is about the serenity that comes when the soul is so deepened that the spirit is naturally gentle.

❧

To lose emotional control over things that have no lasting meaningfulness in life—the speed of the current traffic, the volume of the music, the sound of noise in a public hallway—is a sure sign that the problem is not in the problem. The problem is in me.

❧

There's a phrase for it these days that never shows up in the spiritual manuals but should, maybe: it's called learning to "go with the flow." It means that only God is God, which, of course, relieves the rest of us of a considerable degree of responsibility for the minutiae of life and releases us to be gentle, gentle, gentle.

❧

To be harsh where I could just as easily be gentle is a sign of cirrhosis of the soul, a kind of hardening of the arteries of life. It means the faith I profess is not the faith I really have.

❧

There's no amount of irritation that justifies the loss of self and the battering of the other that masks as strength but is really the most pathetic of weaknesses. The truly strong are the genuinely gentle. They know they are immovable, invulnerable—whatever happens—and so does everyone else.

❧

To be calm in the wake of irritation, to be gentle in the face of annoyance is to hand life over to the impulse of the

Spirit. It allows life to happen in such a way that we can be alive to the surprise in it.

❧

Don't fool yourself that your problem lies in the fact that your life is too busy. People get agitated behind a hay wagon on an empty country road. The question is, What is it inside of us that's driving out the gentleness of spirit that makes beautiful everything that's outside of us?

❧

Gentleness of spirit is more than self-control at a time of anxiety. It is the capacity to embrace the present moment. "Peace," Spinoza said,"is not the absence of war. It is a virtue, a state of mind, a disposition of benevolence, confidence, and justice."

❧

Gentleness of spirit is the gift we give the world in the midst of chaos. It's not passivity and it's not oblivion. It is a continuing consciousness that the little things of life are only that: little.

❧

It's not a matter of waiting until we feel better to be gentle. It's a matter of being gentle in the world around us so that we can feel better. "Inner peace and outer peace are synonymous in the sense, that without one," Yoko Ono said, "the other wouldn't happen."

❧

To argue that someone "made" us angry or the child "made" us irritable or the interruptions "made" us edgy is to argue that we are controlled by something outside ourselves. We are slaves to our environment. We have no control over our thoughts. Nonsense. It's simply the excuse we use to explain why we choose at any given moment to be less gentle than we can be.

⋇

"What it lies in our power to do," Aristotle said, "it lies in our power not to do." So the question is always, What do I get out of doing it? Is it worth the loss of the gentle self?

⋇

Water, Indian wisdom teaches, can only mirror the sky and the trees so long as its surface is undisturbed. The truly spiritual person is the one who realizes that, likewise, we can only be our most human, gentle selves when our minds are at their most tranquil.

⋇

To give in to the self-indulgence of emotional outbursts is to embroil the soul in the negligible and the no-account while the treasures of serenity go ungrasped.

⋇

The worse thing you can say to an agitated person is "calm down." It simply agitates them more. The only answer to agitation is your calmness. If there's no audience for the act, it's useless to stay on stage.

⋇

The really strong of soul are those who are gentle of heart. They have strength in reserve with which to weather the real swells and storms of life. To spill our strength on trivia is to waste it on nothing.

⋇

Outbursts of temper are simply a type of emotional bullying. They are attempts to achieve by manipulation what we refuse to negotiate. They substitute force for strength and weakness for gentleness. They leave us half the person we could be.

❧

"O, it is excellent," Shakespeare wrote, "to have a giant's strength, but it is tyrannous to use it like a giant." Those who are sure of heart can afford to be gentle of spirit. Their strengh is inside of them.

❧

"Anger is an acid," the proverb teaches, "that can do more harm to the vessel in which it stands than to anything on which it's poured." What we are fuming about outside is eating us away inside. What, if anything, is worth the loss of the gentle spirit when what is being corroded is our own well-being?

❧

Gentleness of spirit is what preserves calm in the midst of chaos.

❧

When we were little we sang, "Gentle Jesus, meek and mild . . . " Then, after two world wars, two atomic bombs, and a generation of napalm, the image became very unattractive for women as well as men. So, the spirit of the gentle Jesus has disappeared. And so has peace. Inside and out. I wonder, Has it been worth it?

❧

Assertiveness is a very good thing. It defines persons for themselves. But learning to assert ourselves gently, now there is a task for adults only.

❧

The key to gentleness of spirit is perspective. We must learn to keep small things small before, in their smallness, they consume us.

❧

Whatever "makes" us angry has control of us. Gentleness of spirit is a sign that we have taken back our power.

❧

The body tells us that it likes gentleness. It we're not gentle both with ourselves and with others, we run a high risk of ulcers, heart disease, esophagitis, and headaches. The cure is not another pill. The cure is a spirituality of gentleness.

❧

Gentleness is not innate. It must be learned. It must be developed. It is a virtue to strive for, an attitude to be gained. It is a loving openness toward life.

❧

Abigail Van Buren wrote, "People who fight with fire usually end up with ashes." And actually, that's about all they end up with—if not in the world around them, certainly in their own ungentled hearts.

❧

Gentleness of spirit is the capacity to keep the counsel of the self and remain open to the other at the same time.

❧

Blaming the world around us for the tension we feel is untrue. The world around us seldom changes. It's the tension within us that fluctuates, the gentleness of spirit that comes and goes.

❧

The wag wrote, "There was a time when, if an American missed a stage coach, they just settled down to wait for the next one. Not to worry. There'd be something coming through town in a month or two. Now an American has a breakdown if they miss one section of a revolving door." You can't help but wonder what happened, can you.

IMAGINATION

Genesis 37:19

Here comes that dreamer!

I get a great deal of mail. Most of it I answer, even if only slowly and briefly. So, third-class pieces are almost a relief. They give me a quick glance at the world around me—what people are buying these days, what they're selling, what ideas they're trying to have heard, what they're doing, what gatherings they plan to have. I get a great sense of freedom just being able to skim them and throw them away without having to feel guilty about not writing back.

But I received an invitation from a woman in Florida last year that was clearly polite and clearly not serious at the same time. I had apparently been put on her mailing list haphazardly. I'm not family; I'm not a longtime or even superficially intimate friend—so my presence at the event was clearly not important. I have not been able to forget the invitation, however. I was being invited to her doctoral graduation and the large reception that followed. She was getting a Ph.D. in political science. It was all pretty standard stuff—university commencement, sheepskin, family party—with one exception: the woman who was graduating was eighty years old. What will she ever do with it? you wonder. Foolish, you think. Only if you also think that life is more about career building than soul building. Only if you think that doing is more important than becoming. Only if you think that sinking into diminishment is more natural than growing into dreams at every stage of life.

I didn't answer that letter but I knew that, in one way or another, I'd be responding to it the rest of my life.

❧

Life without a daily dream is not life at all. It is, at best, an excursion into boredom.

❧

There are two ways to live life: flat-footed or flying, plodding or dreaming. When we live flat-footed we simply grind out day after day, doing what must be done and resenting every step of it. When we live life flying, we regard every possible moment as either a step toward our dream for the day or we make it a good time in itself.

❧

My dreams are what drive me on through the humdrum of every day, beyond the obstacles of life to what is not but which I know must be.

❧

What is a dream? It is anything I think should happen and which I, therefore, exert myself to make happen, whatever the odds against it. It is the college education I couldn't get when I was in my twenties but which I am now getting, one night course at a time. It is the new fountain in the garden that I take hours to dig after the regular workday is over. It is the new deck on the home. It is anything that takes an effort that is really no effort at all.

❧

Our dreams keep us going when there is nothing else in life that makes getting up in the morning worthwhile.

❧

A person without a dream is a person for whom life is not living. It is simply the daily death sentence that we have fashioned for ourselves.

᪐

There's a difference between dreaming and fantasizing. A fantasy is something we want to have happen to us without our having to do anything to achieve it. Or, as Sheila Ballantyne put it, "If you have enough fantasies, you're ready—in the event that something happens." A dream, on the other hand, is that great unreachable star in life which we stretch ourselves to grasp.

᪐

What we can imagine we can create: a prison system that rehabilitates rather than incarcerates; an educational system that teaches culture as well as skills; a political system that renounces militarism as its claim to control. "Imagination," Lauren Bacall wrote, "is the highest kite one can fly." What has really happened to the American dream?

᪐

When we cease to imagine the better in life, we sink slowly but inexorably into the mediocre.

᪐

There is no age limit for dreamers. They are simply the people who keep making life better for themselves and for everyone around them.

᪐

The philosopher Simone Weil pointed out that "imagination and fiction make up more than three-quarters of our real life." The question is whether that is a sign that we are looking for dreams or have given them up.

᪐

Life without a dream is life without a direction.

꙳

The dream is everything you can imagine about your own life and then, little by little, set out to make real. A person who does nothing to reimagine his or her own life is a person who has given up on life halfway through it.

꙳

"Heard melodies are sweet," the poet John Keats wrote, "but those unheard are sweeter." Life is good the way it is, of course. But what we imagine it can become is what we must make it, or it is incomplete.

꙳

To imagine "the good life" we need to be able to imagine two kinds of living. One is in prose; the other is in poetry. The problem is that we are inclined to think that life must be one or the other. Actually, life, to be good, must be a balance of the prosaic with an occasional burst of the poetic to keep it fresh.

꙳

Imagination begins when it's raining too hard to go out and play and you become really absorbed in something you would never have thought of doing had the sun come out as usual. In which case, thank God for the rain.

꙳

"Reason can answer questions," Ralph Gerard wrote, "but imagination has to ask them." The important thing is to do something at least once a month you would never have imagined yourself doing: take a day off and go to the zoo, read a few poems whether you understand them or not, attend an opera. Then watch life open up and become new again.

꙳

Imagination is the antidote to becoming sour. We feel our worst when we must find something to do that we have never done before or our sourness will not only paralyze us but poison the environment around us as well.

❧

"One doesn't discover new lands," André Gide wrote, "without consenting to lose sight of the shore for a very long time." To achieve the dream of our lives, we must be willing to let go of the rest of it. Don't smile: letting go takes terrible courage.

❧

Imagination is not idle reverie. It is careful planning and steady progress toward the dream that is doable but doubtful.

❧

The toxin that pollutes the process of getting older is the temptation to give up our dreams. "When we can't dream any longer," Emma Goldman said, "we die." Wrong: we're already dead.

❧

Our dreams are what get us from one finished moment in life to the next one that is trying to be born in us.

❧

Our dreams, the things we imagine that we can be or do or develop, are what we know ourselves to be but have yet to become. And why? Because we simply have not taken that first defining step: register for the course. Change the schedule to include a new activity. Move away.

❧

The ability to imagine different things for ourselves is the one sure sign we have that humans are really made in the image of God.

❧

Imagination and courage are of a piece. It doesn't take a lot of energy to imagine that life will go on as is, but it takes great courage to imagine how we could possibly do something to make it different.

❧

Imagination is the only human faculty that grows with age. As the years go by we collect more and more of the raw material to reimage our lives. The problem with age is simply that, just when we are old enough to realize what could be different, we are also old enough to know what's impossible about it. At that very moment we stop growing. "I admit that twice two makes four is an excellent thing," Dostoevsky wrote, "but if we are to give everything its due, twice two makes five is sometimes a very charming thing, too."

❧

Without people with the ability to imagine a better world, sin smothers the world.

❧

The poet Emily Dickinson wrote:

> *To make a prairie it takes a clover and one bee,*
> *One clover, and one bee,*
> *And revery.*
> *The revery alone will do,*
> *If bees are few.*

It's when we really put our minds to something that life changes. The problem is that we are far more inclined to wait for someone else to change things than we are to imagine what we ourselves might do to cope with it.

❧

Lots of people know lots of things. But, in the end, it's not what we know, it's the way we put things together that makes all the difference. "Imagination is more important than knowledge," Einstein wrote. And he ought to know.

❧

Everything you look at in your life, ask yourself, Should this be different than it is? Then, stop a moment and ask the question that makes imagination sacred. Ask, How? And when you get the answer, do one thing to begin the process.

❧

An American investment banker on vacation in Mexico was trying to make a local fisherman understand that if he fished longer every day he could make more money.

"Ah," the fisherman said, "but if I do that I can't sleep late, play with my children, take a siesta with my wife, and stroll into the village every night to sip wine and play the guitar with my friends."

With that, the American scoffed, "I am a Harvard MBA and could help you. You should spend more time fishing and with the proceeds, buy a bigger boat and with the proceeds from that bigger boat you could buy several boats. Eventually you would have a fleet of fishing boats. Instead of selling your catch to a middleman, you would sell directly to the processor, eventually opening your own cannery. You would control the product, processing, and distribution. You would need to leave this small coastal fishing village and move to Mexico City, then Los Angeles and eventually New York City where you will run your expanding enterprise."

"But how long will this all take?"

To which the American replied, "Fifteen to twenty years."

"But what then?"

The American laughed and said, "That's the best part. When the time is right you would sell your company stock to the public and become very rich. You would make millions."

"Millions? Then what?"

The American answered, "Then you would retire. Move to a small coastal fishing village where you would sleep late, fish a little, play with your kids, take a siesta with your wife, stroll to the village in the evenings where you could sip wine and play your guitar with your friends."

Question: Which of these two guys really had imagination?

QUESTIONING

Luke 2:46

*After three days they found him in the temple,
sitting among the teachers, listening to them
and asking them questions.*

I remember the scene as if it were yesterday. We were a group of teenagers being prepared for confirmation, that Catholic bat/bar mitzvah ritual that carries none of the adult overtones of its Jewish counterpart, but which functions as a kind of Christian rite of passage nevertheless. The parish priest had come in to play bishop, to ask the questions Sister had not, in order to see if we could take the standard catechism answers and make them make sense. In the everyday world, after all, no one asked the questions we'd been reciting by rote for months. If we were going to be defenders of the faith, we would have to be able to answer the real ones. So he asked one.

"Why are you a Catholic?" he said. Hands shot up from one end of the class to the other.

"John," the priest said, pointing to a boy in the front row.

"Because it's the true faith," John said.

"No," said the priest.

"No," I thought. The class paused a minute. Then the hands started to go up again.

"Because all people must be Catholic to get to heaven," Billy said.

"No," the priest said again. You could feel the discomfort set in. The smartest kids turned their eyes away to avoid being called on. "Who else?" the priest asked. "Jane?"

"Because Jesus sent the disciples out to teach all nations."

"No. No. No," the priest said. "Think! Why are you a Catholic?"

"Because I was born Catholic," I said under my breath to the girl next to me, half sniggering, half exasperated.

"Who said that?" the priest asked. "That's right. That's why you're all Catholics. You were born Catholics."

If anything else important happened in that class that day, I don't remember it. I was too busy absorbing this fact.

That day I learned three things that affected the rest of my life: first, that everything, however sacrosanct, was open to questions; second, that every question is an acceptable one; and third, that everything has more than one reason behind it. I learned years later how revolutionary such thinking was. Systems, institutions, ideologies resist questions, forbid questions, for fear the obvious answers undermine the authority of what has always been. But real faith demands questions. Real faith looks under every rock, looks behind every facade, looks through every pallid formula and its pretense at persuasion to find the real face of God and the Jesus who questioned, questioned, questioned everything.

❧

The most subversive thing in life is a question. The courage to ask, Why? has toppled autocracy after autocracy.

❧

When we cease to ask questions we abdicate responsibility for the moral fiber of the moment.

❧

Questions are the gateway to reality. Until we are willing to question the pillars upon which we build our lives, our lives themselves are yet untrue.

❧

People who refuse to question all of the assumptions that underpin the way they live—on the grounds that to ask a question is a violation of faith—are people, ironically, who want cheap answers, not hard faith at all.

❧

Every question in life is an invitation to live with a touch more depth, a breath more meaning.

❧

It isn't what we question that marks us as unsuitable for life's great endeavors, it's what we fail to question. To ask a question simply means that we want to know more about something we consider important; to fail to ask a question that ought to be asked means that we are ignoring human issues for which we should be holding ourselves responsible.

❧

Infant baptism is a lovely gesture. It makes adults feel good and points children in the way they must go. But someday, somehow, every child will find himself or herself back at the baptismal font alone, asking the questions of themselves that once were answered for them, and then having to decide exactly who they are. Why? Because life is not an answer. It is a question beyond all institutional definitions of it.

გა

Without a commitment to ask questions, we may be docile, sociable, and cooperative, but we risk a life without taste, without character, and without wisdom. John Lubock puts it this way: "There are three great questions in life which we have to answer over and over again: Is it right or wrong? Is it true or false? Is it beautiful or ugly?"

გა

Questions go to the core of the present. Answers only satisfy as long as nothing changes. That's why people ask time and time again from childhood on, Do you love me?

გა

Anyone who tries to stop you from asking questions or who won't take no for an answer is trying to control you.

გა

Questions lead us from one stage in life to another. What do I want to be? What am I prepared to be? What is important in life? What do I believe and why? To refuse to honor them is simply to delay our own development.

გა

"The unexamined life is not worth living," Socrates said. In other words, if we don't question ourselves about what kind of person we want to be or about what we really believe, we are living a script—someone else's—not a life.

გა

The "midlife crisis" may, in the end, be nothing more than the reemergence of questions that we failed to ask of ourselves at an earlier stage of life. Am I satisfied with myself?

Do I know why I'm doing what I'm doing? How do I really want to live? Who is God to me?

※

Superficial people are those who simply go along without a question in the world—asking nothing, troubled by nothing, examining nothing. Whatever people around them do, they do, too. That's a sad and plastic life—routine and comfortable maybe, but still sad. "Judge a person by the questions they ask rather than by the answers they give," the philosopher Voltaire once wrote. Think about it.

※

All knowledge comes because someone somewhere refused to accept the answers that were given at face value or asked a question that everyone else took for granted. It gets people rejected socially, of course, as in the feminist revolution. It gets them excommunicated, as with Galileo and Luther. It gets them killed in the race riots of the '60s. But, in the end, it changes life for everyone forever.

※

"If we would have new knowledge, we must get a whole world of new questions," the philosopher Susanne Langer wrote. We must not be afraid to ask anything—no matter who says that the question is not acceptable.

※

To control a person's questions is to stifle his or her conscience.

※

Systems, governments, and institutions are based on answers geared toward their self-perpetuation. That's why questions frighten all of them. "Great evil has been done on earth" Ruby Plenty Chief said, "by people who think they have all the answers."

❧

Some questions don't have answers. Such awareness is the beginning of faith.

❧

"Skepticism," Oscar Wilde wrote, "is the beginning of faith." Until we can begin to unravel what we do not believe, we cannot tell where God begins and we end. We used to think that we were the center of the universe. Now we know that God is bigger than that.

❧

"The skeptic does not mean he who doubts," Miguel de Unamuno wrote, "but he who investigates or researches, as opposed to he who asserts and thinks that he has found." If there were more skeptics in the world, there would be far fewer treason trials and excommunications. Search would be more virtue than heresy.

❧

It is the courage to ask the right questions that makes for moral character. It is the ability to ask the right questions that makes for scientific progress.

❧

No one has a right to ask a critical question to which they themselves are not willing to seek the answer. It is not acceptable, in other words, for me simply to say that I don't like something unless I am willing to say why I don't like it and what, given other information that I have discovered, might be done instead.

❧

Questions are bludgeons and must be asked with great grace for fear of becoming lethal weapons that destroy relationships, people, and well-meaning, even if inept, institutions.

❧

To grow as a person there is one question that is fundamental: "For what reasons might this decision of mine be wrong?" Because I have not pursued all the facts? Because I have not asked the right questions? Because I have not consulted others in the process of forming it? Because I refuse to even think of adjusting to another way of doing things? Because I am too arrogant to even ask the questions?

❧

The axiom "Seldom in doubt, often in error" has its origin in people who refuse to ask questions.

❧

Behind every answer there is another question. Not to deal with it is to avoid the future.

❧

Questions are not simply instruments of social change. They are also agents of social bonding. Sometimes, instead of asking questions of another person, in our panic we talk only about ourselves and then wonder why the person does not respond. Gertrude Stein tells us how to solve the quandary of what question to ask to open a conversation: "How do you like what you have? This is a question that anybody can ask anybody. Ask it." And then watch your social life flower.

❧

Faith is not a commitment to ask no questions. Faith is the capacity to understand that for some things there are no answers, at least not now and not here.

❧

"No one really becomes a fool until they stop asking questions," Charles Steinmetz wrote. And that may be the answer to, How did the world get this way when we weren't looking:

nuclear, pornographic, poor, and oppressive of every minority on earth? If I am part of the problem, and I must be if I have not been part of the solution, then my real conscience question may well be, What questions have I myself been asking and of whom?

❧

"Mother," the little girl camel asked, "why do we have these big three-toed feet?"

And mother camel answered, "So we can walk through the desert without sinking into the sand, love."

The little girl camel thought about that for a minute and then said, "Mother, why do we have these long, thick eyelashes?"

And mother camel answered, "So we can go through desert sandstorms without hurting our eyes, dear."

The little girl camel thought a little more and asked again, "Mother, why do we have these humps on our back?"

And mother camel answered, "So we can walk all the way across the desert without being thirsty, sweetheart."

And the little girl camel said, "Let me get this straight. Our feet are for the desert, our eyelashes are for the desert, and our humps are for the desert. Then will you please tell me what the devil we are doing in the San Diego Zoo?"

Moral: To be in the wrong place, doing the wrong thing at the wrong time is to be a person who didn't ask enough questions of life along the way.

EMOTIONAL STABILITY

John 14:27

*Do not let your heart be troubled
and do not be afraid.*

Being able to be your best self, your calmest self, your most balanced self under pressure is the measure of real psychological and spiritual maturity. There is an old monastic story that gives us all some idea of how far we have yet to go in order to achieve it.

Once upon a time, the story goes, a warlord was terrorizing villages in the hinterland. Stories of his cruelty raced across the mountains and whole villages emptied out before his path in order to escape him. As his litter approached the last of the settlements, he smiled a smug smile and said to one of his soldiers, "The village is empty, I presume."

"Yes, sir," the soldier said. "All of the people have fled before your path—with the exception of one monk who seems to have no fear."

The warlord was aghast. "What!" said the warlord. "Bring the old fool to me immediately. I'll show him what fear is."

When they brought the old monk into the warlord's tent, head high, shoulders back, the tyrant ranted at him, "Do you not know who I am, old man? I am he who can run you through with a sword and never bat an eye."

The old man looked straight into the warlord's eyes and smiled a simple smile. "And do you not know who I am?" he replied. "I am he who can let you run me through with a sword and never bat an eye."

Emotional stability is a learned behavior. We don't "lose" control of our emotions. We choose to let go of our emotions. We do it to punish someone or to get sympathy from someone. We scream at children to control them. We pout at partners to manipulate them. We sob at critics to soften their evaluations. We talk about people "making" us lose our tempers. Then, if we do it often enough, we begin to think that it's natural or necessary. But all the time, it does nothing but diminish the full measure of ourselves, both spiritually and emotionally. It drains our peace.

Real maturity draws from a well of peace that comes from

knowing that God will give us what we need to deal with every situation and the strength that develops from mastering the daily struggle with the self.

❧

It's not what we do under pressure but the way we do it that counts. To react to stress is one thing, to give way to emotional obscenity is another. It only enfeebles us socially and it embarrasses those who must watch us become less than we can be.

❧

It's important to know the kinds of things that tax our serenity most if we're going to be prepared for them when they come. Is it when we're thwarted? Or is it when we're challenged? Or is it when we're confronted? Or it it when we're afraid? Once we know what it is that unsettles us, we can practice responding to it peacefully before it ever happens.

❧

There is no such thing as helplessness. There is only the need to be helpless. The trick is to determine what helplessness provides for us and then set out to provide for it in some better way.

❧

Emotional stability is the capacity to face the winds of contradiction without collapsing under the strain of them. Trust is the bedrock of peace.

❧

Emotional collapse comes when we have given ourselves over to only one part of ourselves. If we concentrate only on the children or only on the job or only on the money, then when the children leave home or the job ends or the money is lost, we have nothing else in life to live for. But when we spend life developing all the many layers of the self, no one thing can possibly destroy us. Peace has a way of seeping from one category to another.

❧

Life is made up of a series of challenges designed to bring us to fullness of growth. Meeting them with hope in the future is the real test of the spiritual person.

❧

The truth is that life is not under our control. So losing control when things go as they will is simply a sign of how great a god we think we are. Annie Dillard says, "We are most deeply asleep at the switch when we fancy we control any switches at all."

❧

Try to remember: If the situation is bad to begin with, then it is bad enough already without our adding to it. Or as the Japanese say, "Cold rice and cold tea are bearable, but cold looks and cold words are not."

❧

People seldom lose control over the big things in life—birth, death, fire, earthquake, flooding. We live through those events, it seems, with great aplomb. It's the little irritations—the late meal, the early meeting, the loud music, the lost remote control—that we use as an excuse to vent our bad feelings all over someone else. The question is Why don't we just talk about what's really bothering us?

❧

It's important to realize that one emotion drives out another. If the anger is beginning to rise in me, it's time to listen to music, to tell a joke, to play with the dog, to paint the back stairs. When we wallow in the negative, we become it.

❧

"We are made kind by being kind," Eric Hoffer said. We become what we do, in other words. If I find myself snapping, snarling, and being generally negative with everyone around me, it's time to wonder whether or not it's not more my fault than theirs.

※

Ambrose Bierce wrote: "In each human heart are a tiger, a pig, an ass, and a nightingale. Diversity of character is due to their unequal activity." Think carefully. Which one have you put in control of your blood pressure today?

※

What mood are you in right now? Why? What are you getting out of choosing it?

※

Moodiness is a person's way of getting attention without having to earn it.

※

"A Puritan's a person," G. K. Chesterton wrote, "who pours righteous indignation into the wrong things." If nobody is listening to you when you lose control, maybe you're losing control over the wrong things. Either that or people are just tired of it.

※

Sometimes we can't do a thing about the situation we're in but we can do something about the way we deal with it.

※

Emotional stability is not an attempt to ignore feelings. It's a commitment to deal with them in ways that harm no one, including one's self.

※

Without emotions we are only half human. Without emotional control, we become more inhuman than human.

꩜

Emotions are the epoxy of human relationships. Only when they become unbalanced do they cloy and kill.

꩜

We have become so "rational" a culture that we have substituted answers for the kind of understanding that can feel the consequences of those answers. Lester Bangs put it this way: "The only questions worth asking today are whether humans are going to have any emotions tomorrow, and what the quality of life will be if the answer is no."

꩜

Emotional stability is not non-feeling; it is the ability to factor feelings into the human equation without being submerged in them.

꩜

Emotions are what qualify us to belong to the human race. It's such an inhuman pity to misuse them. "The young man who has not wept," Santayana says, "is a savage, and the old man who will not laugh is a fool."

꩜

It's as bad to have too little emotion as it is to have too much. The person without emotion is the person without compassion. Compassion comes from the heart, not the head.

꩜

Emotions make us the people we are. To squander them on the inconsequential in great sweeping clouds of rancor and bile and hysteria is to turn them into papier-mache copies of the real thing.

꩜

To say "I took as much as I could and then I couldn't take it any longer and I simply lost control" is to admit that I didn't do something about a thing that bothered me when I should have. As a result, it isn't so much that I "lost" self-control. It's that I gave something with little or no power in and of itself total power over me. It's enough to make a person blush.

❧

It's easy to lie; it's hard to pretend. Unless our emotions are real and not feigned, they will wear thin very quickly.

❧

Life is an exercise in the development of feeling. When we repress feelings, we become sour and judgmental. When we live awash in great feeling over small things, we become jaded long before we have even begun to enjoy. When feelings are in balance they sweeten long days and great distances with gratitude and hope.

❧

It's not reason that makes a person noble and mature. Any robot can figure out facts. It is feelings—in good measure but not in extreme—that make the human being totally human.

❧

Beware people with too little feeling. They are capable of the most heinous of cruelties. Pity people with too much feeling. They are incapable of discriminating between one thing and another.

❧

Emotional stability is not the art of hiding our emotions. It's the ability to deal with them without blowing up airplanes and beating up children and poisoning the environments in which we function. It's having the courage to recognize our feelings, to admit them, and to deal with them without harming either ourselves or anyone else.

PURITY OF HEART

Matthew 5:8

Blessed are the pure of heart; they shall see God.

A good number of things we take for granted never really happen. Instead, the footprints to oblivion are everywhere.

One of the brightest boys I ever taught, for instance—one of those "Most Likely to Succeed" types who got high grades with little study—never did a thing of great merit in life. He moved from position to position and, rather than becoming one of the great academic lights in the country, he eventually settled for an adjunct professorship at a lackluster community college in an eastern backwater. The whole thought of the daily effort it would take to produce high level research material, however naturally capable of doing it he may have been, simply demanded more exertion than he intended to make.

In another place, the local high school basketball team won tournament after tournament only to lose in the finals every year, most people decided, because they consistently underestimated the competition and failed to prepare hard enough to counter anything that happened on the court.

In another case, we had a neighbor who spent her life talking about what she was going to do to take care of her children, to "get on her feet," to start life over again, but though she had good ideas and lots of opportunities, she never did it.

Athletes call such lack of correlation between ability and achievement a case of "not being hungry enough," of not wanting the prize enough to be willing to pay the price it takes to get it. Psychologists use the word *denial* in reference to a person's unwillingness to give an issue the attention it deserves. In the spiritual life, we call a lack of commitment "apathy"— a conscious listlessness, a lack of enthusiasm, a passivity in regard to the important things in life. Monastic literature throughout the ages warns people over and over again about a lack of purity of heart, of the single-minded search for God, whatever the distractions, the seductions, the burdens of life.

In every situation what it really means, as the Irish say, is that we go through life simply "knocking a day out of it." We have nothing we want badly enough or care enough about to concentrate our energies on it.

Then life is, indeed, lackluster, without appetite, lacking direction, gray ashes on gray ground. Then life is dull and meaningless. Then God seems very far away.

Purity of heart is the great white light of life. It is the fuel of commitment. It is what gets us up in the morning and sends us to bed dead tired at night—but smiling.

❧

Wanting something in life and doing what it takes to make it possible are two different things. Either one without the other is only half a life.

❧

When we simply sit around waiting for something to happen, life goes by without our ever having lived it.

❧

Living in such a way that we can become everything God enabled us to be is what makes the daily delicious.

❧

"A virtue to be serviceable must, like gold," Samuel Butler wrote," be alloyed with some commoner but more durable metal." All the talent in the world, all the goodwill on earth, is useless unless it is wedded to the "more durable metal" of the burning, single-minded commitment that is purity of heart.

❧

The Chinese say, "When we don't know where we're going, any road will get us there." Purity of heart is the ability not to be deluded by less than the ultimate reality of life itself.

❧

Everything in life is important but not everything is equally important at the same time. It's not possible to tell one from the other, however, unless we first know ourselves.

❧

Purity of heart—the laser beam of the soul—is what enables us to choose between goods in life. It's always easy to choose between good and evil. It's choosing between two goods that is difficult.

❧

To have purity of heart is to go through life, magnet in hand, looking for the clearest path to fulfillment.

❧

"Human improvement," Froude wrote, "is from within outward." It's when we think that the fullness of life comes from outward within that we start making choices that slow down our development.

❧

What we take as our ideals in life determines who and what we will become. Ask yourself who your heroes are and you will know what you really want out of life, all public proclamations to the contrary.

❧

Whatever it is that drives us—profit, power, pleasure, the presence of God—determines all our choices in life. That can be bad, of course, but at least it is clear. To be driven by nothing is no small problem of its own.

❧

To know the degree of purity of life in a person, simply ask them what they are willing to give up to get what they say they want. Then ask yourself the same question. If you can't think of anything, think again.

❧

"My strength," Tennyson wrote, "is as the strength of ten, because my heart is pure." Only when we want something badly enough can we rise to possibilities beyond ourselves.

❧

Purity of heart concentrates human energy, strips away what is useless, foregoes aimlessness, and puts us on the straight-and-narrow path to fulfillment. Athletes and lovers are the best proof we have that the transcendent is possible.

❧

Unless we want something badly enough to make changes in our own lives to get it, it is doubtful that we really want it at all.

❧

Purity of heart and singleness of purpose are opposite sides of the same coin. Everybody is centered single-mindedly on something: on family, on work, on leisure, on money, on something! The only difference is that those who are pure of heart in the classical sense are centered on the "ultimates" of life, on God, goodness, love, justice, and wholeness of heart. I'm spiritually mature when I begin to ask myself, What's my center?

❧

To have no priorities in life is to have no life at all, no basis for decision making, no principles to steer by.

❧

To know what drives me it is only necessary to listen to the self. Down deep inside a tape plays in all of us that tells what is really absorbing us. Some people can go through life without ever taking the time to pay attention to the voice of the soul. Then they wonder why they're always disappointed in life.

❧

"The spirit points in a certain direction," John Cassian wrote. "There is an unwavering purpose in the mind." Everybody has one. It colors everything we do and determines our every choice. Until we ourselves know what it is, we can't possibly deal with it.

❧

"When the drunk goes into a temple," the Sufi say, "it becomes a place of pollution. And when the monk goes into a bar, it becomes a temple." Whatever we want at the center of ourselves shapes the environment around us.

❧

Purity of heart, the magnet of the soul, leads us to the Source of ourselves.

❧

"For those who travel without a marked road," the sage said, "there is the toil of the journey—and no arrival at a destination." Purity of heart is knowing what we're about in life. Really about.

❧

The pure of heart are those who seek God in everything and who never fail to find the presence of God everywhere.

❧

The real athletes, the real prophets, the real achievers are those who never, under any circumstances, allow themselves to be distracted from the goal. First, of course, you have to know what it is. "Aye, there's the rub," as Shakespeare says.

❧

To be pure of heart is to fall prisoner to nothing less than the highest goals of the human spirit.

❧

Purity of heart is not about being asexual. It is about being totally committed to the only thing worth being really committed to: the fullness of spiritual development in a highly material age.

❧

"Blessed are the pure of heart," Scripture reads, "for they shall see God." Blessed are those who spend their lives looking for God, in other words. We can't possibly see that which we have no intention of finding in the first place.

❧

The pure of heart are those who "keep their eyes on the prize." The saddest thing of all is not to have a prize big enough to be worth getting.

❧

To go through life without a sense of direction is, in the end, only to dabble in it, to wait for something better to come along. And it never does, of course, because we wouldn't know it if it did.

❧

The pure of heart purify their lives of whatever it is that distracts the heart from its true home.

❧

One night a wife found her husband, a woodworker, standing over their newborn baby's crib. As the woman watched her husband looking down at their sleeping infant, she saw on his face a mixture of emotions: delight, amazement, enchantment, total disbelief.

Touched by this unusual display and the deep emotions it aroused, she slipped her arms around her husband, her eyes glistening. "A penny for your thoughts, darling," she whispered in his ear.

"I just can't believe it!" he gasped. "I just can't see how anybody can make a crib like that for only $46.50!"

Now that's single-mindedness.

INCLUSION

John 17:22–23

*The glory that you have given me I have given
them, so that they may be one, as we are one,
I in them and you in me, that they may become
completely one.*

I t was a typical Italian night and the sky was going from
rose to black. Up on the top of a rocky bluff overlooking
the Mediterranean Sea, I could see the lights of the village. Down on the strand where we were, the last of the local
diners were strolling lazily out of tiny cafes as a warm wind
curled through the narrow streets at the foot of the mountain.
I don't remember where we'd been. All I know is that we got
back later than planned, the lights up and down the mountain were going out one at a time, there was no food in the
little garret at the top of the walk-up flat, and we were hungry. "How much money do you have?" I asked her. "Don't
worry," she said. "I have a credit card."

It was after we'd ordered that I thought to ask about the
card in my slow and halting Italian.

"No, no, no signora," the owner answered, shaking his
head decisively.

"No?" I asked with all the incredulity I could muster to
make it perfectly clear that these were not the ways of the
civilized world.

"No, signora," he repeated, eyelids drooping in the style
of the best Italian regret.

"He doesn't take credit cards," I said to her while he stood
there, pencil poised. "We'll have to order again but remember, I only have 8,500 lira. That's about $7.00. That's about
enough for soup and bread and salad. No wine." We gave one
another a tight grimace and picked up the menus once more.

"No, no, no signora," he said again, this time waving his
arms over the old order form with great broad strokes. "Mangia
tutto." Eat everything. "Pagami domani." Pay me tomorrow.

"Domani," I thought. Tomorrow? This man doesn't even
know us. Why would he ever think that we would come back
tomorrow to pay for food we'd eaten tonight? Surely, he doesn't
mean that.

But he did mean it. And we did eat. And we did drink.
And, on top if it all, his nephew drove us home at almost

midnight just to make sure that the two American signoras got there safely.

That, I thought later as I wrote in my journal, is a glimpse of the perfect world, the kind of which the Book of Revelation dreams. That is inclusion. And because of that night and that man—not because of its great art, not because of its churches and basilicas, not because of its ancient ruins—Italy sings in my heart yet today.

❧

It isn't that we don't leave out anybody that marks us as truly human. It's that we don't take everybody in that makes the difference between civility and humanity. It's easy to be civil. It's holy to be inclusive.

❧

"The fact that we are human beings," Simone de Beauvoir wrote, "is infinitely more important than all the peculiarities that distinguish human beings from one another." The great spiritual question is Why do ethnic, social, sexual, and class differences tend to separate us more than the notion of a shared humanity unites us? When we get that answered, the world will be at peace and the gospel will have been preached.

❧

Inclusion is a good thing when it erases differences, and a bad thing when it suppresses identity.

❧

Never doubt that the people with whom we associate are what we are. They are, in fact, the measure of our own real community to human community. The kind of people we include in our lives are images of what we ourselves want to be, which is why, all our mothers told us to "be careful who your friends are."

❧

"Of my two 'handicaps,'" Representative Shirley Chisholm wrote, "being female put many more obstacles in my path than being black." Ouch. Tell me again how far we've all come?

❧

It's what we are keeping out of our private little worlds that describe the scope of our interest and our understanding.

✢

To be a loner is to stop our education. It is when we learn from others in life that we are really stretched beyond our own imaginings.

✢

Whatever is the most other, most unlike thing, in my life is exactly what I need to get to know. After all, it represents the part of me that has yet to be developed.

✢

Who is it that I would not have at my dinner table? It might be a sad commentay on the quality of their lives. But the problem is that it may be an even sadder commentary on mine.

✢

"Rabbi," the disciples said, "surely you aren't going to give another coin to that beggar? He will only waste it."And the rabbi said, "But should I be more finicky about giving it to him than was the God who gave it to me?" It's so easy to read others out of deserving the really worthy things of the world and so easy to read ourselves into them. Let's hope we're all reading as God reads.

✢

"The test for whether or not you can hold a job," Bella Abzug said, "should not be the arrangement of your chromosomes." Now that we know that we share similarities with some of the lowest creatures on the planet, being male, female, human isn't half the justification for arrogance, prejudice, or sexism that is used to be.

✢

"It is extremely difficult to like oneself in a culture which thinks you are a disease," Chrystos writes. The problem is that people full of self-hatred, because we all judge everybody else by our definition of ourselves, find it impossible to love others, too. So the cycle of hate simply goes on and on. In the end, it may be exclusion, not militarism, that is the world's most terminal social disease.

❧

If so many people are to be sorted out of my life, why ever in heaven do you suppose God made them in the first place? Who is really strange here: God, the stranger, or I?

❧

Exclude anyone you want from your little kingdom now, but as you do, remember the words of the Roman statesman, Seneca: "Injustice never rules forever"—and take cover.

❧

How do you separate the acceptable from the unacceptable in a person anyway? Or, as Groucho Marx, put it: "Since my little daughter is only half Jewish, would it be all right if she went into the pool only up to her waist?"

❧

When we admit what it is that we exclude from our ideal world and then determine why that is, we come face to face with the inadequacies in ourselves. It is what I exclude that challenges the limitations in my own personality.

❧

The persons, the groups, who are other than I am are the people who most widen my view of the world.

❧

What if there really are other—even better—ways of being in the world? Then, how would I possibly know if I were really right or not, really deserved to be in charge or not, really were the ideal or not? Ideas like that could change sexism, could destroy racism, could eliminate discrimination, could turn our worlds upside down.

❧

Remember one time in your life when you felt excluded. Why were you being excluded? Was it fair? Was it right? What did you learn from it? Really? How would anyone know?

❧

Taking the strange idea, the strange person, the strange place into our lives makes us bigger than we are.

❧

The world of the self is a small world indeed. And very dull company besides.

❧

All the borders of the world are open. The question is, Are the borders of the heart big enough to take the strain?

❧

To what groups, clubs, associations do you belong? What are the membership rules in each of them? Why? What have you done about it? Why?

❧

Difference and inequality are not the same. Difference enriches us; inequality enslaves both the keeper and the kept.

❧

Think of it: the black who is not allowed to be black in our presence unless he or she sounds, talks, and dresses white; the woman who is not allowed to be a woman in a system unless she takes on the expectations of men; the young male artist who is considered psychologically suspect unless he flaunts his machismo, all buy inclusion for too dear a price. And as long as that lasts, the rest of us get our feelings of human decency all too cheaply.

❧

Sometimes we exclude things in ourselves in order to be like everybody else around us—our ethnicity, our social backgrounds, our ideas. What kind of world is it that will not allow me to be myself, and is it really good for me to be there? What part of me will die a slow death if I stay?

❧

Until we trust a stranger, we have not trusted anyone.

❧

To exclude anyone on the basis of sex, race, sexual orientation, or religion from the confines of my world is to make myself a very small god of a very small territory.

❧

It isn't easy to reach out to the person who is totally other than I am in language, background, color, sex, ideas. But it is the only totally human act of which I am capable.

❧

Put down all the categories in your life—liberal, conservative, heterosexual, homosexual, color, gender, and religion. Now, what's left? I call it Mickey Mouse theology: as in "It's a small, small world." You might also—if Canaanite, Samaritans, women, Roman soldiers, and Pharisees count as "others"—call it Christian. There's a thought.

NATURE OF THE HEROIC IN LIFE

Wisdom 3:7

The upright shall shine forth,
and will run like sparks through stubble.

S aints"—spiritual heroes of character and courage—are very elusive figures and not always all too comfortable ones either. They carry with them the ideals of ages often quite remote from our own, even, in some cases, psychologically suspect now. They seem to uphold a standard of perfection either unattainable to most or, at least in this day and age, undesirable to many. Their lives are often overwritten, their struggles underestimated, and their natural impulses underrated. They have become a rather quaint anachronism of an earlier church, full of simpler people far more unsophisticated, we think, than ourselves and whom we think ought to be quietly ignored in these more enlightened times. I disagree.

The fact is that in a culture full of drugged-up rappers, drunken athletes, obscenely glittering celebrities, and street gang members dangling with body rings and covered with violent tattoos, real heroes seem to be thin on the ground. We could use a saint or two, perhaps, to raise our sights again to the heights of human possibility and the depths of the human soul. It might not even hurt to pass on one or two of them to children who are otherwise left with little to choose from as personal idols than what Hollywood, TV, and the music industry have already given them, of course.

I knew a saint once: he was a young man with an old grandmother, a sick mother, and two brothers in wheelchairs as a result of a genetically inherited illness. He stayed home, unmarried, and devoted his entire life to care for each of them, one at a time, all the way to the grave. His inspiration didn't come from stars or American glitterati. It came from saints, the heroes of the daily.

ॐ

Heroes are people who do ordinary things—care for people, speak the truth, reject evil, love God, seek the truth—to an extraordinary degree. All of history is full of their struggles, their triumphs: Eve, the mother of the human race, gives men and women everywhere an appreciation for intelligence and a warning about its misuse.

ॐ

"You cannot be a hero without being a coward," George Bernard Shaw wrote. The university martyrs of El Salvador were academics who believed that ideas could change things even in a repressive regime. To protect themselves from a murderous government, they did everything possible to draw attention to their cause. They were assassinated nevertheless but to the end they were true to the ideals of the gospel. That's sanctity, and those were heroes.

ॐ

"The purpose of prayer, my daughters," Theresa of Avila wrote, "is always good works, good works, good works." Given her heroic and unending attempts to make religion spiritual and the church holy, she, of all people, had the right to say so. She did not use prayer as a refuge, she used it as a beacon. Learning to persist in the pursuit of good would make saints of us all.

ॐ

"What is a society without a heroic dimension?" Jean Baudrillard asked. Charles de Foucauld, the Christian saint who lived a heroic life of loneliness and deprivation among the Arabs simply to be a sign of love to them from a part of the world they feared, did not try to erect a system that would save the world. He just set out heroically to save the part of it where he was.

❧

Hagar, the handmaiden driven into the desert by the jealousy of Sarah and the weakness of Abraham after she gave Abraham the heir Sarah could not, is a heroic model for the abandoned and rejected today. She brings with her a sense of the God who resides in the resilient and unbreakable heart and teaches us all how to hang on when hanging on seems neither possible nor desirable.

❧

Mother Jones, the Irish-American woman who gave her entire life to the organization of day laborers, was, at the age of eighty-eight, still hard at work reshaping the American labor movement. She is a clear sign that no season of life is too late to give the gift of conscience. No generation is without responsibility for the sins of its times. She dreamed of a better world and she set out to get it. That's heroism. That's sanctity.

❧

Oscar Romero, the conservative bishop of El Salvador who became radicalized by the plight of the poor under the country's oppressive regime, discovered that the gospel supersedes the church. Most of all he said so, despite the church's traditional support for government positions, or at least their silence in the face of them. It was a heroic position to take and, in the end, they murdered Romero but it turned the tide of public opinion and eventually the political situation itself. "Heroism, however useless it seems, always leaves a light for others to follow," said Lord Byron.

❧

Mary Magdalene is the woman who sees God and summons others to see him, too, in a culture where women summoned no one anywhere. She is a heroic model of what it means to live life whole and full of confidence in the God who made us.

❧

"In this life of illusion and quasi-illusion," Daniel J. Boorstin wrote, "The person of solid virtues who can be admired for something more substantial than his well-knownness often proves to be the unsung hero." We all know heroes; we simply fail to recognize them because we have substituted admiration for eccentricity rather than character.

❧

Julian of Norwich, a fifteenth-century anchorite who was devoted only to God in an age devoted largely to things, gave the world three "learnings" that would change the very things we call holy: that God is mother, that fear of God is not humility, and that even though we sin all will be well. Those are brave, heroic concepts in a world where God, who is all spirit, has been reduced to the notion of a male judge.

❧

"Unhappy the land that is in need of heroes," wrote Bertolt Brecht. And every day the crime sections of our newspapers prove the point.

❧

What Dorothy Day—convert, unmarried mother, and founder of Catholic Worker House for the desperately poor—raised out of the ashes of her life is a monument to living. She was the kind of hero that everyone else, anyone else, can be, not by changing other people but by changing themselves.

❧

What we have come to call heroic is violence in behalf of violence. Our public parks hold statues of military figures from more or less glorious wars. As the poet Byron wrote:

> *The drying up of a single tear has more*
> *of honest fame than shedding seas of gore.*

If we want new kinds of heroes we will need to raise statues to Florence Nightingale and Madame Curie and Dorothy Day, all of whom spent their lives helping others, not killing them.

❧

Charles Horton Cooley wrote: "To have no heroes is to have no aspiration, to live on the momentum of the past, to be thrown back upon routine, sensuality, and the narrow self." Ask yourself who your heroes are and you will know something more about your own character.

❧

Francis of Assisi touched the soul of a newly rich century with a sense of conscience for the world to contemplate for ages to come. In Francis, the world gets a bewitching glimpse of mighty powerlessness. It is a heroism beyond violence, beyond power, light years beyond the plastic privileges of affluence. It calls us to see our own strength, raw and unadorned.

❧

Clare was a woman who insisted that women who followed Francis be allowed to live the same radical poverty that the men did. It was an idea unheard of for women who had no way to beg, no chance to earn. It is the radical, the heroic, among us who make us look again at the nature and function of religion and what it does to us and what we do to it.

❧

Rumi the Persian was a poet-mystic. He is a poignant voice from the thirteenth century who taught about love and the nature of life and union with God long before those were common coin in a hard world where money counts more than character.

❧

Martin of Tours gathered a community of men around him whose whole lives stood in direct opposition to the male military values of the world in which they had been formed. They were a searing reminder of the gentle, loving, saving Christ. It was a heroic stand against the war philosophies of both church and state.

❧

Simone Weil was defined as one of the most important spiritual thinkers of the age. She offers a silent invitation to take into the twenty-first century a healthy distrust of everything about it so that no ideology, no institution may seduce us into believing that any system is enough for us. It takes great heroism to question every element of life—for fear we may come to think differently than the world says we ought.

❧

Pedro Arrupe, a Jesuit superior general who led the order's transition to Vatican II theology, had two serious problems. First, Arrupe called the sign of the time justice and saw thirty-three Jesuits assassinated in behalf of their work for the poor. Second, his style of leadership was collegial rather than authoritarian. He simply could not bring himself to suppress the movement of the Holy Spirit among his brothers in the name of obedience to the system. And so he lost favor with the Vatican. But both his heroic insights live on.

❧

The life of Catherine of Siena is a thunderclap that vibrates yet. The legacy of Catherine of Siena to the twenty-first century is that she lived an intensely private life of Christian service, gospel commitment, Christian feminism, and patient prophetism. It was the kind of heroism that makes every new day more worth living than the one before it.

❧

The Baal Shem Tov was a man with an eye for the spiritual and a song in the heart. Nothing clearly authentic is known about him but nothing much has been forgotten about the man either. The Baal Shem Tov insisted that the presence of God lurked in life as it was, that it was there for the seeing, that to live life joyfully was itself the real task of life.

❧

Thomas Merton became a heroic archetype of Christian conscience at a time of the Vietnam War and Christian salvation through the here and now. He left three legacies: the Christian vocation to peacemaking, a respect for Eastern monasticism in the Western world, and a renewed understanding of the role of the religious vocation in the public arena.

❧

The Rule of Benedict seeded the elements that were later credited with having "saved Western civilization." Benedict of Nursia stood in the midst of a decaying society and refused to go into decay with it. He showed the world a better way to live by living it sanely and deeply every day. What can be more heroic for any of us?

❧

"Heroes are created by popular demand," Gerald Johnson wrote, "sometimes out of the scantiest materials." We will get in heroic figures what we demand. When Christ is the ideal, society begins to look loving and compassionate and open. When money and power and escapism are the ideal, we get the macho, the cheap, and the crude. Don't complain. Choose.

❧

Martin Luther King, Jr., waged one long unending campaign for the soul of the century. In the end he did not simply save African Americans, he saved the very moral fiber of the country and the hope of oppressed peoples everywhere.

❧

John XXIII is really remembered for making human that which is political, scholarly, efficient, clerical, and papal. What stands as a monument to his heroism is the indictment of ageism by an old man who turned a system upside down to make it new again. Now, thanks to him, age is no excuse for doing nothing.

❧

Franz Jagerstatter chose for conscience in a Nazi society and paid for it with his life. For him, the most important thing a father had to do for his children was to be a holy man, a heroically holy man, and he showed it to the end.

❧

Hildegard of Bingen left a legacy that is yet to be inherited by the human race. She is everything that both women and men are, at long last, discovering women in general to be: inspired, intelligent, fearless, and, indeed, called by God. She was, in other words, a very heroic woman in an age when women were considered less than whole persons. That type of heroism is needed now more than ever.

❧

With a voice to lead them, a path to follow, and a goal to pursue, the oppressed came from every side to join Mahatma Gandhi in his nonviolent pursuit of human freedom. Gandhi asks us to critique government and law according to a higher power. He reminds us to be patient with others, to do no one harm, to pursue truth with heroic passion.

❧

Joan of Arc's heroic commitment to conscience over authority is a mighty one. There are some things in life that belong to God alone, Joan implies: human life, human responsibility, human will. Joan of Arc is patron of all those who hear the voice of God calling them beyond present impossibilities to the fullness of conscience everywhere.

The meditations in this book come from Sister Joan Chittister's monthly spirituality sheet *The Monastic Way,* 2000 edition. For subscription information, please contact:

BENETVISION
355 East Ninth Street
Erie, PA 16503-1107
Phone (814) 459-5994
Fax (814) 459-8066
www.eriebenedictines.org